Rookie
Read-About® Health

of

Mexico City • New Delhi • Hong Kong
Danbury, Connecticut

Designer: Herman Adler Design
Photo Researcher: Caroline Anderson
The photo on the cover shows a girl getting an eye exam.

Library of Congress Cataloging-in-Publication Data

Curry, Don L.
　Take care of your eyes / Don L. Curry.
　　p. cm. — (Rookie read-about health)
　Includes index.
　ISBN 0-516-25874-5 (lib. bdg.)　　　　　0-516-27914-9 (pbk.)
　1. Eye—Care and hygiene—Juvenile literature.　I. Title. II. Series.
　RE52.C875 2005
　617.7—dc22
　　　　　　　　　　　　　　　　2004015302

What do you see in this picture?

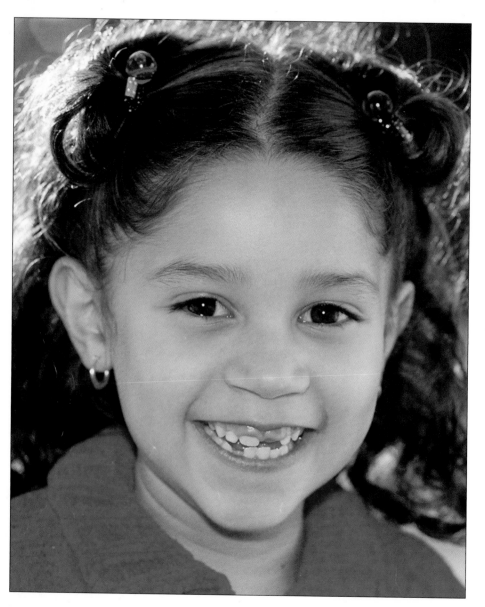

4

What did you use to see those things?

You used your eyes! Your eyes are amazing. They help you see all the things you need to see.

You use your eyes to help you play. You use your eyes to help you draw pictures. You use your eyes to help you write, too.

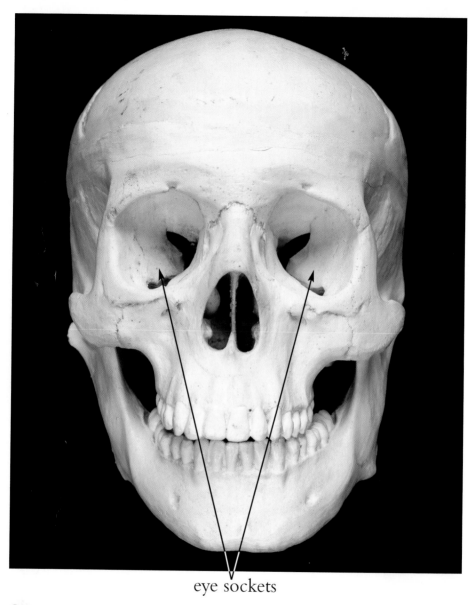

eye sockets

Your eyes sit in small holes in the front of your head. These holes are called eye sockets.

The hard bones of your head protect your eyes.

Your eye has different parts. Your iris is the colorful part of your eye. Your pupil is the black circle in the middle.

pupil   iris

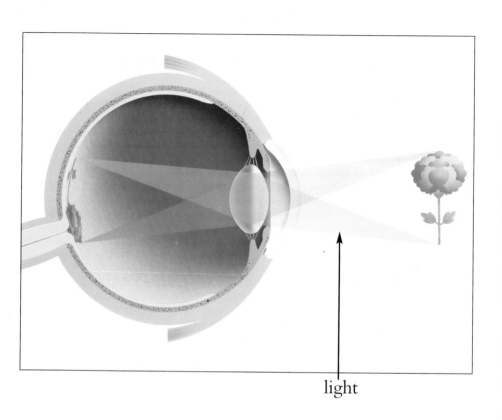

light

Your pupil opens to let in light. The light passes through your pupil until it reaches a nerve in the back of your eye.

The nerve sends messages to your brain. These messages tell your brain what you are seeing.

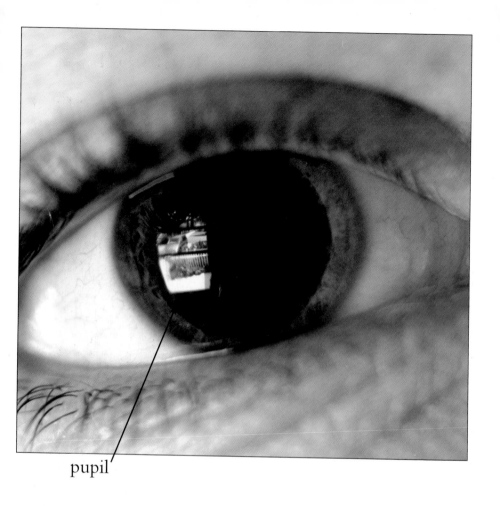

pupil

Your pupil opens wide
when it is dark.

Your pupil gets smaller in bright light. This protects your eyes from too much light.

pupil

You should protect your eyes.

Never look directly at the Sun. Always wear sunglasses on a sunny day.

What else protects
your eyes?

Your eyelids do! They
keep your eyes clean
and moist.

eyebrow　　　　　　eyelash

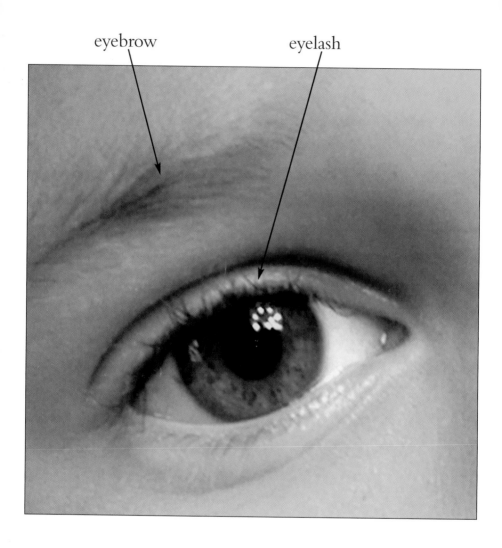

Your eyebrows and eyelashes help protect your eyes, too.

They help to keep out dust.

If something does get in your eyes, ask an adult for help.

Do not rub your eyes. You might hurt them.

Be sure to protect your eyes when you play sports.

These girls wear goggles when they swim.

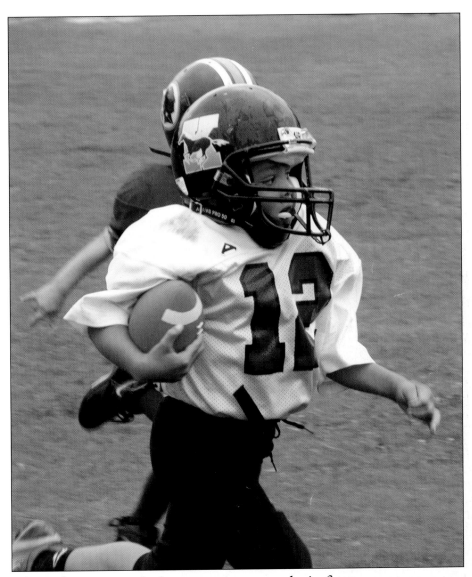

These boys wear helmets to protect their faces.

An eye doctor can look at your eyes.

The doctor may give you glasses to help you see better.

Take good care of
your eyes.

There is a lot to see in
the world!

Words You Know

eye doctor

eyelashes

eyelids

goggles

iris

pupil

sunglasses

Index

About the Author

Don L. Curry is a writer, editor, and consultant who lives and works in New York City. He has written more than 30 nonfiction books about science. The study of the human body is by far his favorite topic. When Don is not writing, he can be found reading in Central Park or riding his bike on the streets of "the greatest city on Earth."

Photo Credits